Monitoring Whitebark Pine in the Greater Yellowstone Ecosystem

2011 Annual Report

Natural Resource Data Series NPS/GRYN/NRDS—2012/278

Greater Yellowstone Whitebark Pine Monitoring Working Group

Bozeman, MT 59715

April 2012

U.S. Department of the Interior
National Park Service
Natural Resource Stewardship and Science
Fort Collins, Colorado

The National Park Service, Natural Resource Stewardship and Science office in Fort Collins, Colorado publishes a range of reports that address natural resource topics of interest and applicability to a broad audience in the National Park Service and others in natural resource management, including scientists, conservation and environmental constituencies, and the public.

The Natural Resource Data Series is intended for the timely release of basic data sets and data summaries. Care has been taken to assure accuracy of raw data values, but a thorough analysis and interpretation of the data has not been completed. Consequently, the initial analyses of data in this report are provisional and subject to change.

All manuscripts in the series receive the appropriate level of peer review to ensure that the information is scientifically credible, technically accurate, appropriately written for the intended audience, and designed and published in a professional manner. This report received i peer review by subject matter experts who were not directly involved in the collection, analysis, or reporting of the data.

Views, statements, findings, conclusions, recommendations, and data in this report do not necessarily reflect views and policies of the National Park Service, U.S. Department of the Interior. Mention of trade names or commercial products does not constitute endorsement or recommendation for use by the U.S. Government.

This report is available from http://science.nature.nps.gove/im/units/gryn/.index.cfm and the Natural Resource Publications Management website (http://www.nature.nps.gov/publications/nrpm/).

Please cite this publication as:

Greater Yellowstone Whitebark Pine Monitoring Working Group. 2012. Monitoring whitebark pine in the Greater Yellowstone ecosystem: 2011 annual report. Natural Resource Data Series NPS/GRYN/NRDS—2012/278. National Park Service, Fort Collins, Colorado.

NPS 960/113528, April 2012

Contents

Figures

Tables

Abstract

Whitebark pine (*Pinus albicaulis*) occurs at high-elevations and in subalpine communities in the Pacific Northwest and Northern Rocky Mountains. It is a key component in the upper ranges of these ecosystems where it provides a variety of ecological roles, including regulating runoff by slowing the progress of snowmelt and providing high energy food sources to birds and mammals. As a stone pine species, it produces indehiscent cones and relies primarily on birds for seed dispersal.

Whitebark pine, in mixed and dominant stands, occurs in over two million acres within the six national forests and two national parks that comprise the Greater Yellowstone Ecosystem. Currently, whitebark pine is being impacted by multiple ecological disturbances. White pine blister rust (*Cronartium ribicola*), mountain pine beetle (*Dendroctonus ponderosae*), and wildfires all pose significant threats to the persistence of healthy whitebark pine populations on the landscape. Substantial declines in whitebark pine populations have been documented throughout its range. Since 2004, an interagency effort has resulted in a monitoring protocol and a complete sampling frame of data. The objectives of the whitebark pine monitoring program are to detect and monitor changes in the health and status of whitebark pine populations across the GYE due to infection by white pine blister rust, attack by mountain pine beetle, and damage by other environmental and anthropogenic agents. This report presents a summary of the data collected between 2008 and 2011.

Acknowledgments

We thank our current and past field technicians John Fothergill, Adam Morris, Chad Hockenbary, Carson Lindbeck, David Brodhead, Rachel Simons, Jennifer Birdsall, Polly Buotte, Justin Hof, Karla Sartor, Jonathan Ball and Amy Jesswein. We thank former Greater Yellowstone Network ecologist Rob Bennetts for his contribution to the sample design and development of the monitoring protocol, and Steve Cherry from Montana State University for ensuring statistical validity to the sampling regime. We also thank Cathie Jean, Karrie West, Nancy Bockino, Andy Pils, Bill Oliver, Megan Higgs, Jamie Thornton, Katie Banner, Marcus Engler, Ellen Jungck, and Karl Buermeyer for their advice and/or field and logistic support. Seed funding for this program was provided by the NPS Greater Yellowstone Inventory & Monitoring Network. Additional funding and in-kind support for this program is provided by USFS Forest Health Monitoring, USGS (Interagency Grizzly Bear Study Team), the Greater Yellowstone Coordinating Committee (GYCC), the US Fish and Wildlife Service, the US Forest Service, and from Yellowstone and Grand Teton National Parks.

Members of the Greater Yellowstone Whitebark Pine Working Group include:

Jodie Canfield, Forest Biologist
USDA Forest Service
Gallatin District, Gallatin National Forest

Gregg DeNitto, Forest Pathologist
USDA Forest Service
Forest Health Protection

Jay Frederick, Subcommittee Chair
USDI Greater Yellowstone Coordinating Committee
Whitebark Pine Subcommitee

Mark Haroldson, Acting Study Team Leader
Shannon Podruzny, Study Team Ecologist
USDI Geological Survey
Interagency Grizzly Bear Study Team

Kathi Irvine, Statistician
USDI Geological Survey

Kristin Legg, Program Manager
Rob Daley, Data Manager
Erin Shanahan, Project Coordinator/Crew Leader
USDI National Park Service
Greater Yellowstone Inventory and Monitoring Network

Kelly McCloskey, Vegetation Ecologist
USDI National Park Service
Grand Teton National Park

Dan Reinhart, Resource Manager
USDI National Park Service
Yellowstone National Park

Dave Roberts, Department Head
Montana State University
Department of Ecology

List of Acronyms

BR   blister rust

CI   confidence interval

DBH   diameter at breast height

GRYN   Greater Yellowstone Inventory & Monitoring Network

GYCC   Greater Yellowstone Coordinating Committee

GYCCWPS   Greater Yellowstone Coordinating Committee Whitebark Pine Subcommittee

GYE   Greater Yellowstone Ecosystem

GYWPMWG   Greater Yellowstone Whitebark Pine Monitoring Working Group

IGBST   Interagency Grizzly Bear Study Team

MPB   mountain pine beetle

MSU   Montana State University

NPS   National Park Service

RZ   Recovery Zone (grizzly bear)

SE   standard error

USFS   United States Forest Service

USGS   United States Geological Survey

Introduction

Whitebark pine (*Pinus albicaulis*) occurs at high-elevations and in subalpine communities in the Pacific Northwest and Northern Rocky Mountains. It is a key component in the upper ranges of these ecosystems where it provides a multitude of ecological functions, including regulating runoff by slowing the progress of snowmelt and providing high energy food sources to birds and mammals. Whitebark pine often grow in locations that are inhospitable to other tree and vegetative species, though once it has populated an area, it creates favorable habitat that enables other species to colonize. By generating these beneficial microenvironments, whitebark pine plays a significant role in forest successional processes and promotes diversity (Tomback and Kendall 2001). As a stone pine species, it produces indehiscent cones and relies primarily on birds for seed dispersal (McCaughey and Schmidt 2001). High in calories and rich in fat, these seeds provide seasonal forage for a variety of wildlife. In addition to its ecological importance in high elevation ecosystems, whitebark pine is a revered icon for backcountry explorers and mountain recreationists.

Whitebark pine, in mixed and dominant stands, occurs in over two million acres within the six national forests and two national parks that comprise the Greater Yellowstone Ecosystem (GYE) (Greater Yellowstone Coordinating Committee Whitebark Pine Subcommittee [GYCCWPS] 2010). Currently, whitebark pine is being impacted by numerous ecological disturbances. Substantial declines in whitebark pine populations have been documented throughout its range. White pine blister rust (*Cronartium ribicola*), mountain pine beetle (*Dendroctonus ponderosae*), and wildfires all pose significant threats to the persistence of healthy whitebark pine populations on the landscape.

Interagency Whitebark Pine Monitoring Program

Under the auspices of the Greater Yellowstone Coordinating Committee (GYCC), the National Park Service Inventory and Monitoring Program and several other agencies began a collaborative, long-term monitoring program to track and document the health and status of whitebark pine across the GYE. This alliance resulted in the formation of the Greater Yellowstone Whitebark Pine Monitoring Working Group (GYWPMWG), which consists of representatives from the U.S. Forest Service (USFS), National Park Service (NPS), U.S. Geological Survey (USGS), and Montana State University (MSU). A protocol for monitoring the health and status of whitebark pine populations in the GYE was developed between 2004 and 2007 by the GYWPMWG. After rigorous peer review, the Interagency Whitebark Pine Monitoring Protocol for the Greater Yellowstone Ecosystem (GYWPMWG 2011) received final approval in 2007 and was recently updated in 2011. A complete protocol is available at: http://www.greateryellowstonescience.org/subproducts/14/72.

This report presents a summary of the data collected by the monitoring program between 2008 and 2011.

Monitoring Objectives

Generally, the objectives of the whitebark pine monitoring program are to detect and monitor changes in the health and status of whitebark pine populations across the GYE due to infection by white pine blister rust, attack by mountain pine beetle, and damage by other environmental and anthropogenic agents.

Specifically, the Interagency Whitebark Pine Monitoring Protocol (GYWPMWG 2011) addresses the following four objectives:

Objective 1 - To estimate the proportion of live whitebark pine trees (>1.4 m tall) infected with white pine blister rust, and to estimate the rate at which infection of trees is changing over time.

Objective 2 - Within transects having infected trees, to determine the relative severity of infection of white pine blister rust in whitebark pine trees >1.4 m tall.

Objective 3 - To estimate survival of individual whitebark pine trees >1.4 m tall explicitly taking into account the effects of white pine blister rust infection rates and severity, mountain pine beetle activity, fire, and other damaging agents.

Objective 4 – To assess and monitor recruitment of whitebark pine understory individuals (<1.4 m tall) into the cone producing population (a pilot effort was initiated in 2010 and will be implemented in 2012).

Stud ' Area

The study area is wi hin the GYE and includes six natio ial forests a id two national parks (the John D. Rockefeller Memorial Parkway is included wit Grand Teton National Park) (Figure 1). The target populatio i is all whitebark pine trees in the GYE. The sa nple frame includes stands of white ark pine approximately 2.5 ha or greater withi i and outsid of the grizzly bear Recover y Zone (RZ). A total of 10,770 mapped whitebark polygons or stands were identified in the map ing process with 2,362 located within the RZ and 8,408 located outside of the RZ. Stands ithin the R were derived from the cumulative effects model for grizzly bears while outside the RZ, the sample frame includes whitebark stands mapped by each of the six separate USFS u its and compiled by the NPS for the cumulative effects mo lel effort (Dixon 1997, pers. com. L. Landenburger, 2012). Areas that burned since the 1988 fires were excluded from the sample frame.

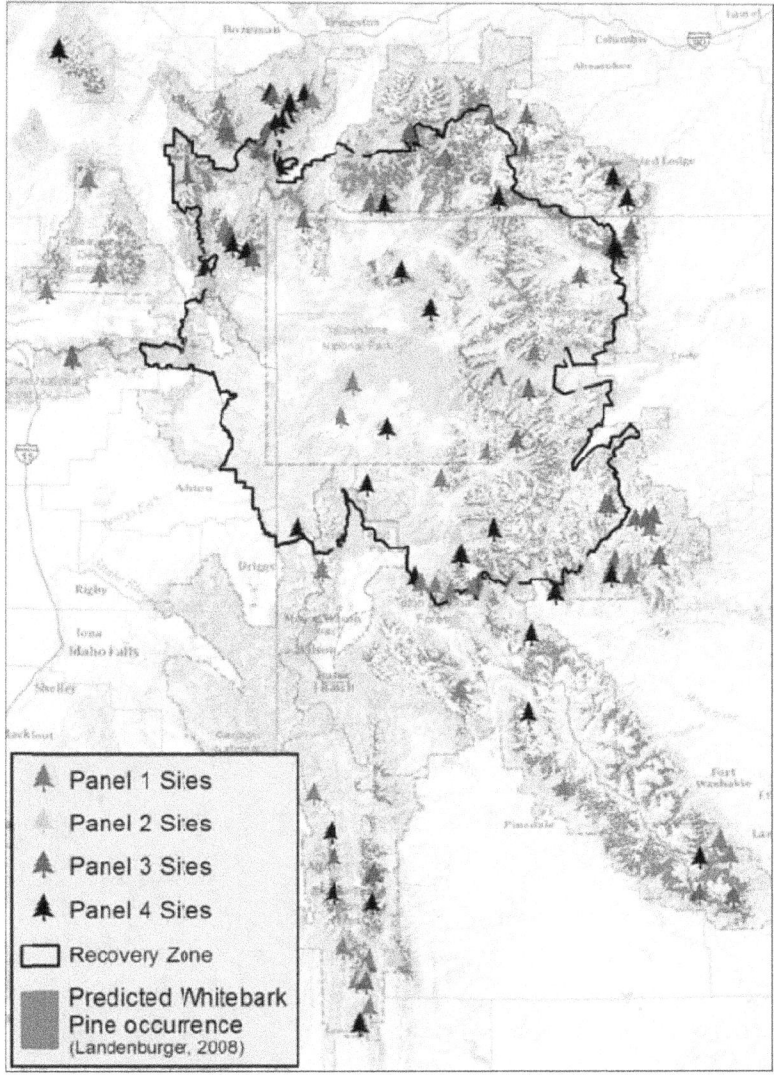

Figure 1. Location of whitebark pine survey transects, Greater Yellowsto ie Ecosystem. Panel 1, 2, 3, and 4 ha l a full resurvey for white pine blister rust infection in 2008, 2009, 2010, and 2011 respectively.

Methods

Details of the sampling design and field methodology can be found in the Interagency Whitebark Pine Monitoring Protocol for the GYE (GYWPMWG 2011) and in past program reports (GYWPMWG 2005, 2006, 2007, 2008, 2009, and 2010). The basic approach is a two-stage cluster design with stands (polygons) of whitebark pine being the primary units and 10x50 m transects being the secondary units. Initial establishment of permanent transects took place between 2004 and 2007; during this period 176 permanent transects in 151 whitebark pine stands were established and 4,774 individual trees >1.4 m tall were permanently marked in order to estimate changes in white pine blister rust infection and survival rates over an extended period. The sample of 176 transects is a probabilistic sample that provides statistical inference to the GYE.

In 2008, individual transects were randomly assigned to one of four panels; each panel consists of approximately 44 stands. This is the number of transects that can be realistically visited in a given field season by one, two-person field crew. Sampling every four years is sufficient to detect change in blister rust infection; however, with the recent increase in whitebark pine mortality due to mountain pine beetle, the monitoring group became concerned that a four year revisit interval might not be sufficient to document the timeliness of overall mortality of whitebark pine trees > 1.4 m tall. In response, we temporarily modified the revisit design to incorporate the dynamic nature of the current mountain pine beetle epidemic to a two-year revisit schedule. With this design, two of the four panels are surveyed annually; one panel is subject to the full survey documenting white pine blister rust infection and mountain pine beetle indicators while the second panel is subject to a partial survey focused solely on mountain pine beetle indicators (Figure 2). Both surveys record tree status as live, dead, or recently dead.

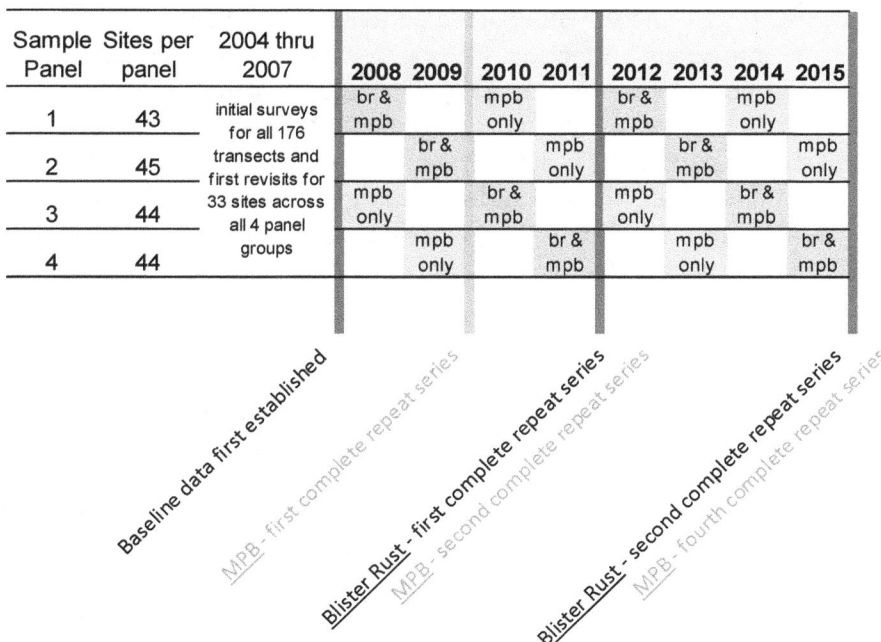

Sample Panel	Sites per panel	2004 thru 2007	2008	2009	2010	2011	2012	2013	2014	2015
1	43	initial surveys for all 176 transects and first revisits for 33 sites across all 4 panel groups	br & mpb		mpb only		br & mpb		mpb only	
2	45			br & mpb		mpb only		br & mpb		mpb only
3	44		mpb only		br & mpb		mpb only		br & mpb	
4	44			mpb only		br & mpb		mpb only		br & mpb

Baseline data first established — MPB - first complete repeat series — Blister Rust - first complete repeat series — MPB - second complete repeat series — Blister Rust - second complete repeat series — MPB - fourth complete repeat series

Figure 2. Panel sampling revisit schedule. Although revisits are scheduled for mountain pine beetle through 2015, this is dependent on available funds and length of the outbreak.

Eighty-five transects were resurveyed in 2008, 90 in 2009, 88 in 2010, and 87 in 2011 by two, two-person crews, one led by the NPS Greater Yellowstone Inventory & Monitoring Network (GRYN) and the other led by the USGS Interagency Grizzly Bear Study Team (IGBST).

Full Survey: White Pine Blister Rust and Mountain Pine Beetle Surveys

From 2008 to 2011, panels 1, 2, 3, and 4 have been revisited once for white pine blister rust (BR) and twice for mountain pine beetle (MPB). The presence or absence of white pine blister rust infection was recorded for all live trees in each panel. For the purpose of analyses presented here, a tree was considered infected if either aecia or cankers were present. For a canker to be conclusively identified as resulting from white pine blister rust, at least three of five ancillary indicators needed to be present (GYWPMWG 2011). Ancillary indicators of white pine blister rust included flagging, rodent chewing, oozing sap, roughened bark, and swelling (Hoff 1992). For each live tree, pitch tubes and frass were recorded as evidence that the tree had been infested with mountain pine beetle. Pitch tubes are small, popcorn-shaped resin masses produced by a tree as a means to stave off a mountain pine beetle attack. Frass or boring dust is created during a mountain pine beetle attack and can be found in bark crevices and around the base of an infested tree. Bark is removed from dead trees to expose the J-shaped galleries that are present in an attack and indicate where adult mountain pine beetle and their larvae live and feed (GYWPMWG 2011).

Mountain Pine Beetle Only/Mortality Survey

For mountain pine beetle only/mortality surveys, data are collected solely on mountain pine beetle indicators. As described above, each live tree is examined for pitch tubes and frass while all dead trees are investigated for J-shaped galleries.

Recruitment and Understory Individuals

During the full survey, all ≤1.4 m tall whitebark pine trees on a given transect are counted and observed for white pine blister rust infection. Once a tree has reached a height greater than 1.4 m tall, it is permanently tagged and assessed in a manner consistent with all other live, marked trees in the sample frame. In 2011, pilot efforts were initiated to assess and monitor recruitment of whitebark pine understory individuals (≤1.4 m tall) into the cone producing population. Once we have completed the statistical consultation and peer review process, methods for detecting trends in the understory population of whitebark pine will be incorporated into the protocol (GYWPMWG 2011) and implemented in 2012.

Analysis Methods

The proportion of trees infected with white pine blister rust is calculated using a design-based ratio estimator that accounts for the total number of mapped stands within and outside the grizzly bear RZ (GYWPMWG 2011).

The GYWPMWG continues to investigate the role of observer variability in white pine blister rust (Huang 2006) and mountain pine beetle detection. Each field season, a minimum of 25% (approximately 10) of the full white pine blister rust survey transects are subject to the double observer survey described in the protocol (GYWPMWG 2011). Information gleaned from these records allows us to correct problems through improved training, hiring, and retention of trained and experienced field crew members. If observer variability is found to be a major contributor to the standard error for the estimated parameters, we will assess this in the data analysis.

Results

Status of white pine blister rust

The 2007 baseline estimate of the proportion of live whitebark pine trees infected with white pine blister rust in the GYE is 0.20 (±0.037 se) (GYWPMWG 2008). This estimate is based on data from 4,774 individual live trees in 176 transects collected over a four-year period between 2004 and 2007 after all transects and tree records were established. In Table 1, we report the estimates of the proportion of whitebark pine trees infected with white pine blister rust based on the resurveys of panels 1, 2, 3, and 4 conducted in 2008, 2009, 2010, and 2011 respectively. The estimates for proportion of live trees infected only infer to each panel for the year they are resurveyed. It should be recognized that these estimates do not denote a cumulative proportion of live trees infected from 2008 to 2011.

Upon completion of the 2011 field season, all panels were resurveyed once for white pine blister rust infection. From these combined data between 2004-2007 and 2008-2011, we will present a step-trend analysis on white pine blister rust change, severity of infection, and survival of whitebark pine in the GYE. This analysis effort is underway and anticipated to be complete in 2012.

White pine blister rust infection remains widespread throughout the ecosystem. Decreases in white pine blister rust infection observed on some transects are most likely an artifact of increased mortality on the transect due to mountain pine beetle infestation or wildfire. Increases in white pine blister rust infection are explained by the actual increase in observable infection on trees within a transect.

Status of tree survival

To determine whitebark pine mortality, we resurvey all transects to reassess the status of permanently tagged trees >1.4 m tall. We subtract the total number of resurveyed dead tagged trees from the total number of live tagged trees recorded during initial establishment period from 2004 to 2007. By the end of 2011, we observed a total of 977 dead tagged whitebark pine trees within the boundaries of the permanent monitoring transects; this equates to a loss of approximately 20% of the original live tagged tree sample (see Figure 3). While transects are experiencing varying degrees of mortality, they are also experiencing varying degrees of recruitment. Once a whitebark pine tree within the transect boundary reaches a height greater than 1.4 m tall, it is permanently tagged and included in the live tree sample. As of 2011, 3,767 (79%) of the originally marked trees remained alive, 30 trees were not relocated (1%), and an additional 301 new trees were added (Table 2).

Table 1. Design based ratio estimates for the proportion of infected whitebark pine trees >1.4 m tall in panel 1, 2, 3 and 4 and other summary information (Irvine 2010).

2008 [Panel 1] Location	Within Recovery Zone	Outside Recovery Zone	Total for Panel 1
Number of stands	15	22	37
Number of transects	15	27	42
Number of unique trees sampled	323	661	984
Number of transects infected	13 of 15	19 of 27	32 of 42
Proportion of live trees infected	0.137	0.281	0.249
Proportion of live trees infected Standard Error (SE)	0.055	0.037	0.031
Confidence Interval (CI) for proportion of live trees infected	[0.018, 0.255]	[0.205, 0.357]	[0.186, 0.312]
2009 [Panel 2] Location	Within Recovery Zone	Outside Recovery Zone	Total for Panel 2
Number of stands	17	21	38
Number of transects	17	28	45
Number of unique trees sampled	295	684	979
Number of transects infected	13 of 16	26 of 28	39 of 44
Proportion of live trees infected	0.16	0.465	0.398
Proportion of live trees infected Standard Error (SE)	0.066	0.062	0.051
Confidence Interval (CI) for proportion of live trees infected	[0.019, 0.300]	[0.336, 0.595]	[0.296, 0.501]
2010 [Panel 3] Location	Within Recovery Zone	Outside Recovery Zone	Total for Panel 3
Number of stands	16	22	38
Number of transects	16	29	45
Number of unique trees sampled	370	675	1,045
Number of transects infected	11 of 16	24 of 29	35 of 45
Proportion of live trees infected	0.128	0.102	0.108
Proportion of live trees infected Standard Error (SE)	0.042	0.07	0.055
Confidence Interval (CI) for proportion of live trees infected	[0.037, 0.218]	[-0.043, 0.248]	[-0.005, 0.220]
2011 [Panel 4] Location	Within Recovery Zone	Outside Recovery Zone	Total for Panel 4
Number of stands	16	21	37
Number of transects	18	26	44
Number of unique trees sampled	168	1022	1190
Number of transects infected	16 of 18	25 of 26	41 of 44
Proportion of live trees infected	0.23	0.25	0.25
Proportion of live trees infected Standard Error (SE)	0.118	0.073	0.062
Confidence Interval (CI) for proportion of live trees infected	[-0.017, 0.485]	[0.097, 0.400]	[0.119, 0.372]

Table 2. Mortality and recruitment status of whitebark pine trees from 2008-2011 that were marked in 2004-2007. The new recruits were not included in the calculations of the proportion of dead and live trees.

2004-2007 transect establishment	2008-2011 resurvey results				
Live trees tagged	Total dead trees (from original 4,774 tagged)	% dead tagged trees	% live, tagged trees	% tagged trees not relocated	New recruits added (not included in percentages)
4,774	977	20%	79%	1%	301

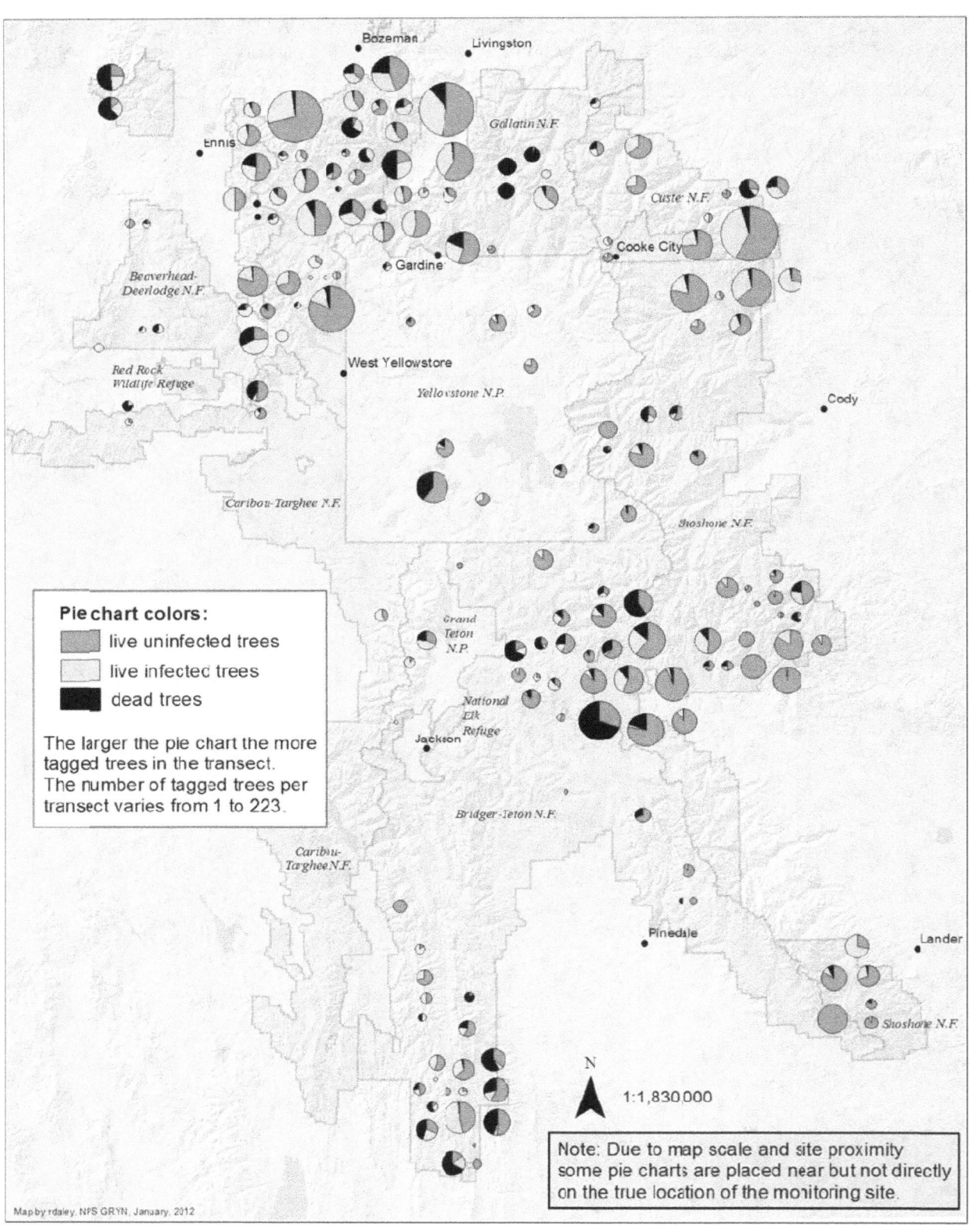

Figure 3. Preliminary map of the ratio of whitebark pine trees within each transect as alive, dead or with the presence of blister rust infection from surveys 2004-2011. The infection status ranges from a tree with a single canker on a branch to a tree that may have a bole canker.

10

Presence of mountain pine beetle

High elevation forests across the GYE are experiencing elevated mortality as a result of the current mountain pine beetle epidemic. Mountain pine beetle exhibit a propensity for attacking whitebark pine trees that are 10 cm DBH and greater. Trees that are equal to or less than 10 cm DBH are not large enough to successfully support mountain pine beetle brood (Amman et al. 1977); consistent with this observation, tree mortality observed in transects was much greater in trees >10 cm DBH. By the end of 2011, we found that 33% (n=775) of the trees >10 cm DBH had died, whereas only 8% (n=202) of the trees ≤10 cm had died (Figure 4).

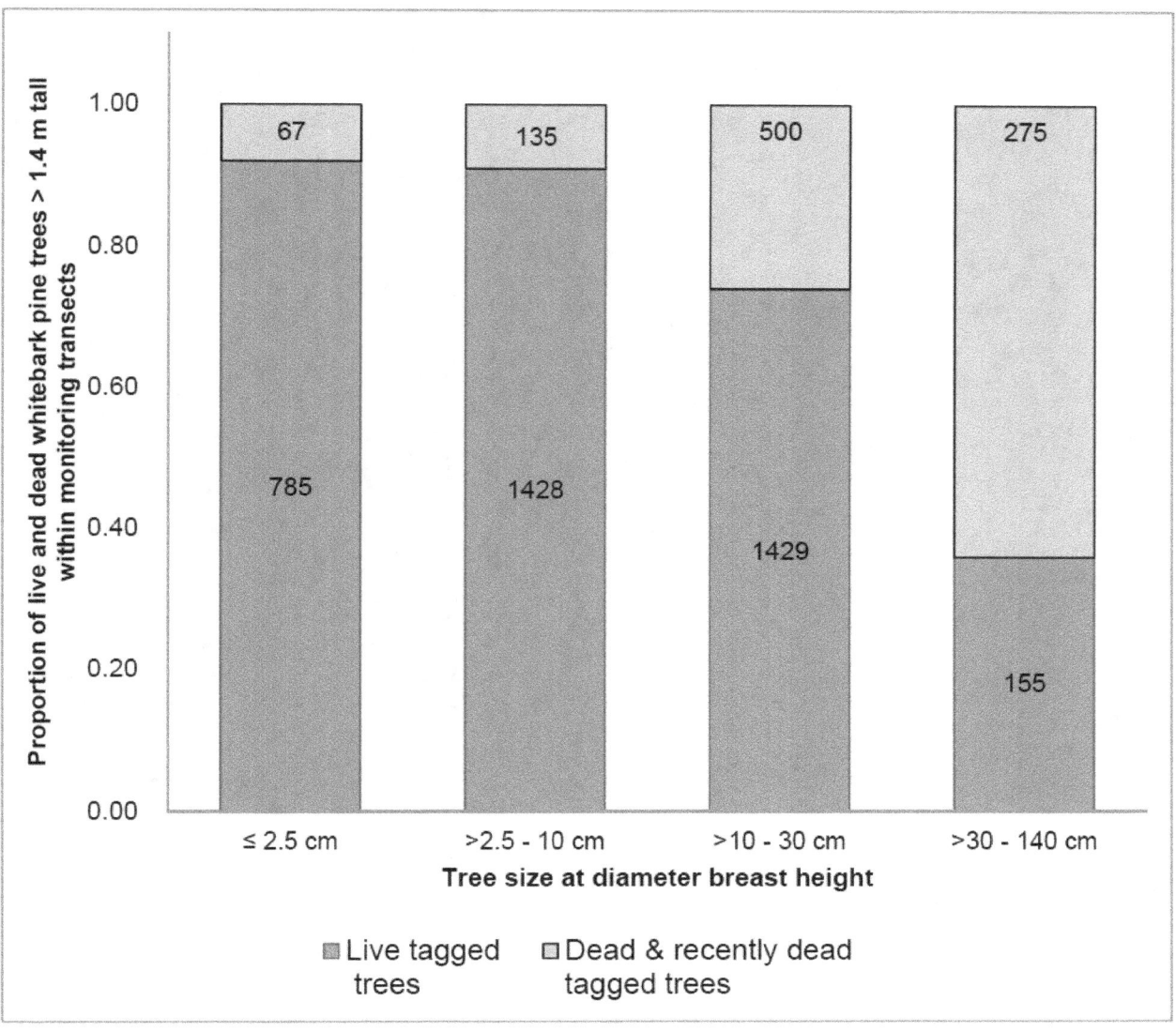

Figure 4. Proportion of live, dead, and recently dead tagged whitebark pine >1.4 m tall within the monitoring transects by size class at the end of 2011. A recently dead tree has persistent non-green needles, whereas a dead tree has shed all of its needles. These values are based on the original sample (4,774) and do not include the 301 trees that have been added since initial establishment. Dead and recently dead could be from any number of causes such as mountain pine beetle, fire, windthrow, or unknown.

Of the resurveyed trees that were recorded as dead since initial transect establishment, approximately 71% had J-shaped galleries present underneath the bark. Similar to white pine blister rust infection, mountain pine beetle infestation is widespread and varies in severity throughout the GYE. Of the 176 established transects, 111 have recorded evidence of mountain pine beetle infestation while 65 have no observed evidence of mountain pine beetle infestation (Figure 5).

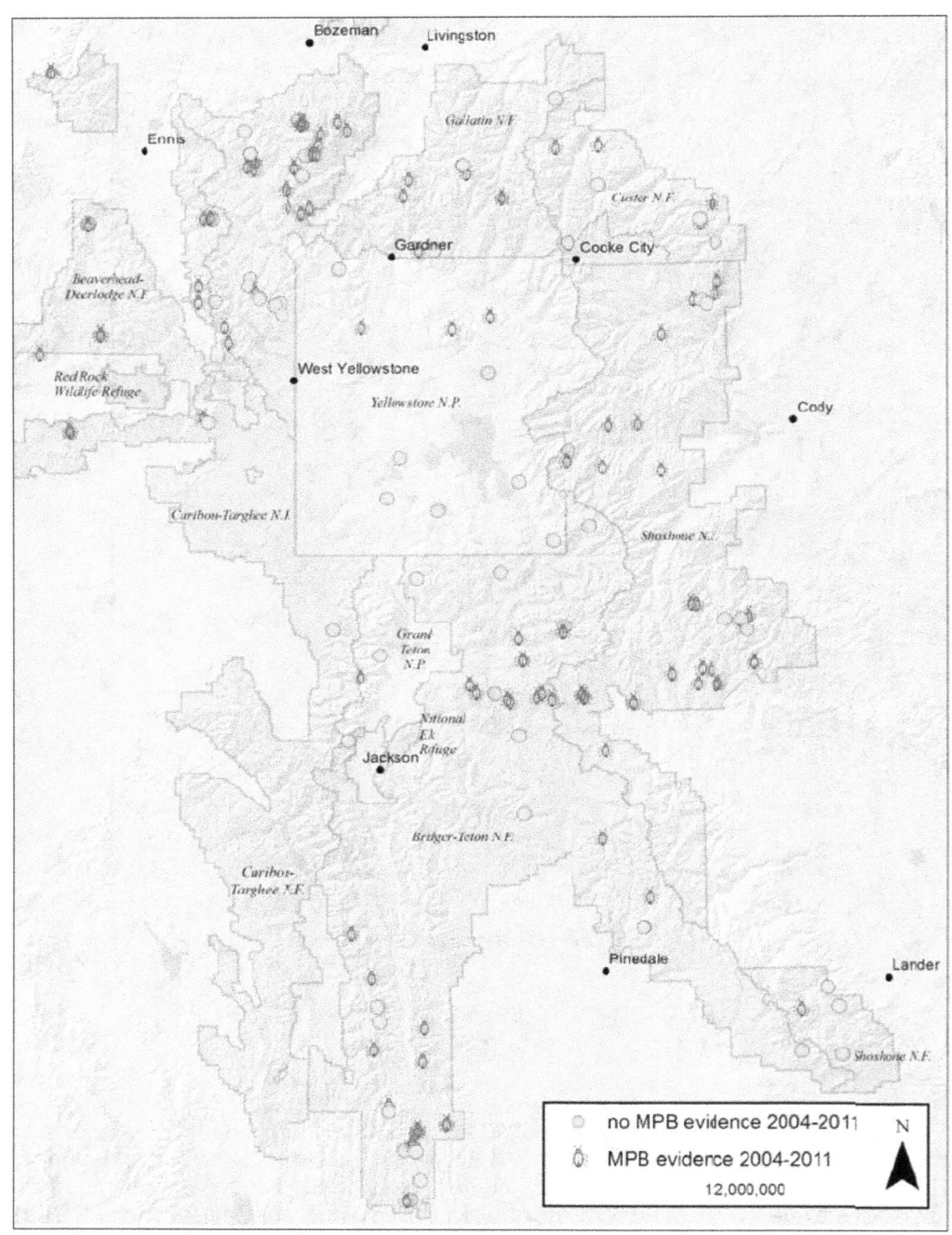

Figure 5. Location of transects throughout the Greater Yellowstone Ecosystem with and without evidence of mountain pine beetle infestation.

Future Direction

This year, 2012, will mark the beginning of the second complete revisit of panels 1 through 4 following the panel revisit schedule in Figure 2. In addition, we will commence implementation of Objective 4 of the protocol to assess and monitor the recruitment of whitebark pine understory individuals into the cone producing population as well as collect baseline data on whitebark pine demographics. In 2012, we will be preparing a step-trend analysis of data collected between 2004 and 2011.

This long-term monitoring program provides critical information that will help determine the likelihood of whitebark pine persisting as a functional and vital part of the ecosystem. In addition, data from this program are currently being used to inform managers, guide management strategies and restoration planning, and substantiate conservation efforts throughout the GYE. The interagency protocol has also been a valuable resource for a variety of agencies embarking on five-needle pine monitoring including the Greater Yellowstone Coordinating Committee's Whitebark Pine Strategy for the Greater Yellowstone Area (GYCCWPS 2011).

Literature Cited

Ammen, G. D., McGregor, M. D., Cahill, D. B., Klein, W. H. 1977. Guidelines for reducing losses of lodgepole pine to the mountain pine beetle in unmanaged stands in the Rocky Mountains. USDA For. Serv. Gen. Tech. Rep. INT-36, 19 p. Intermt. For. and Range Exp. Stn., Ogden, Utah 84401.

Dixon, B. G. 1997. Cumulative Effects Modeling for Grizzly Bears in the Greater Yellowstone Ecosystem. Thesis Montana State University. 143 pages plus appendices. Bozeman, Montana, USA.

Greater Yellowstone Whitebark Pine Monitoring Working Group. 2011. Interagency Whitebark Pine Monitoring Protocol for the Greater Yellowstone Ecosystem, Version 1.1. Greater Yellowstone Coordinating Committee, Bozeman, Montana, USA.

Greater Yellowstone Whitebark Pine Monitoring Working Group. 2010. Monitoring Whitebark Pine in the Greater Yellowstone Ecosystem: 2009 Annual Report. Pages 56-65 in C. C. Schwartz, M. A. Haroldson, and K. West, editors. *Yellowstone Grizzly Bear Investigations: Annual Report of the Interagency Grizzly Bear Study Team*, 2009. U.S. Geological Survey, Bozeman, Montana, USA.

Greater Yellowstone Whitebark Pine Monitoring Working Group. 2009. Monitoring Whitebark Pine in the Greater Yellowstone Ecosystem: 2008 Annual Report. Pages 62-68 in C. C. Schwartz, M. A. Haroldson, and K. West, editors. *Yellowstone Grizzly Bear Investigations: Annual Report of the Interagency Grizzly Bear Study Team*, 2008. U.S. Geological Survey, Bozeman, Montana, USA.

Greater Yellowstone Whitebark Pine Monitoring Working Group. 2008. Monitoring Whitebark Pine in the Greater Yellowstone Ecosystem: 2007 Annual Report. Pages 50-56 in C. C. Schwartz, M. A. Haroldson, and K. West, editors. *Yellowstone Grizzly Bear Investigations: Annual Report of the Interagency Grizzly Bear Study Team*, 2007. U.S. Geological Survey, Bozeman, Montana, USA.

Greater Yellowstone Whitebark Pine Monitoring Working Group. 2007. Monitoring Whitebark Pine in the Greater Yellowstone Ecosystem: 2006 Annual Report. Pages 46-54 in C. C. Schwartz, M. A. Haroldson, and K. West, editors. Yellowstone Grizzly Bear Investigations: Annual Report of the Interagency Grizzly Bear Study Team, 2006. U.S. Geological Survey, Bozeman, Montana, USA.

Greater Yellowstone Whitebark Pine Monitoring Working Group. 2006. Monitoring Whitebark Pine in the Greater Yellowstone Ecosystem: 2005 Annual Report. Pages 73-80 in C. C. Schwartz, M. A. Haroldson, and K. West, editors. *Yellowstone Grizzly Bear Investigations: Annual Report of the Interagency Grizzly Bear Study Team*, 2005. U.S. Geological Survey, Bozeman, Montana, USA.

Greater Yellowstone Whitebark Pine Monitoring Working Group. 2005. Interagency Whitebark Pine Health Monitoring Program for the Greater Yellowstone Ecosystem, 2004 Annual

Report. Pages 92-125 in C.C. Schwartz, M. A. Haroldson, and K. West, editors. *Yellowstone Grizzly Bear Investigations: Annual Report of the Interagency Grizzly Bear Study Team*, 2004. U.S. Geological Survey, Bozeman, Montana, USA.

Greater Yellowstone Coordinating Committee Whitebark Pine Subcommittee. 2011. Whitebark Pine Strategy for the Greater Yellowstone Area. 41p. Greater Yellowstone Coordinating Committee. Bozeman, MT, USA.

Hoff, R. J. 1992. How to recognize blister rust infection on whitebark pine. USDA Forest Service, Intermountain Research Station, Research Note INT-406, Ogden, Utah., USA.

Huang, M. 2006. A Statistical Analysis of Observer Variability in the Identification of Blister Rust Infection Occurring in White-Bark Pine Monitoring. Unpublished Report prepared for the Whitebark Pine Monitoring Working Group. Department of Mathematical Sciences, Montana State University, Bozeman.

Irvine, K. 2010. Greater Yellowstone Network: Status estimates for white pine blister rust. Report in partial fulfillment for RM CESU Task Agreement. National Park Service, Greater Yellowstone Network, Bozeman, Montana, USA.

McCaughey, W. W. and W. Schmidt. 2001. Taxonomy, distribution, and history. Pages 29-40 in D. F. Tomback, S. F. Arno, and R. E. Keane, editors. *Whitebark Pine Communities: Ecology and Restoration*. Island Press, Washington, D.C. USA.

Tomback, D. F. and K. C. Kendall. 2001. Biodiversity losses: The downward spiral. Pages 243-262 in D. F. Tomback, S. F. Arno, and R. E. Keane, editors. *Whitebark Pine Communities: Ecology and Restoration*. Island Press, Washington, D.C.